Dedication

This book is to all those, women and men who struggle to believe God has made them somebody. To all those who have gone through constant hurt and pain believing they aren't worthy of God's love, this book is for you.

Be blessed.

Acknowledgements

First and foremost, I want to thank my Saviour, my Lord, my doctor, my everything, Jesus Christ who has held me, kept me, nurtured and cared for me when there was no one else around. He never ever let me go, no matter how many times I turned away. He has always protected and provided for me. I thank Him for His ever present intercession and protection on my behalf. For carrying me through my times of depression and sorrow, for always showing me I am worth something to Him and Our Father above.

To my children, Jacole, Juanita, and Timothy, for always loving me, believing in me and dealing with me when I was grouchy and sleepy. You guys are everything to me. We have truly been through some rough times. You are awesome. We have shed a lot tears and shared even more smiles. Without you three in my life, I don't know what I would do. God has blessed me with stewardship over the three of you and I'm going to do my very best to do well by all of you. I love you all very much

To all the children that have come into my life that God has given to me spiritually, this book is to show all of you that, as long as you believe and live the way God tells you to no matter what things will come to pass. There are so many of you I don't want to put names but all of my sons and daughters through adoption, all I love each and everyone of you.

To my parents, I've tried to honour you. At times I haven't done the best job, but I am proud to say that I do have two of the best parents in the world. We may not agree on everything, but I know you care for and love me very much and I thank you for that. Thank you both for the correction and discipline; even when I didn't want it. It has helped make me a better person. I love you two very much.

To my brothers; Keith and William, my sisters; Angel and Courtney, thank you for ears that listened when I needed them. May God bring all of you true happiness and joy. May He show you all the true meaning of love, happiness and a peace that passeth all understanding.

Uncle Bryan, you are the absolute bomb. You never doubted me; you always encouraged me, guiding me along the way. Gosh, God did something awesome when He put you in my life. I love you because, in your eyes, I will always be N'Tantala, the twelve year old little girl, who always wanted to chill with her Uncle BeeBri. I love you.

To all my friends who have encouraged me along the way, my God-brother Tony, told ya everything is going to work out. To my cousin and friend Leeann, you always made sure you were there for me. I love you girl.

To my Asian sister Rita, my girl Tascha, My sisters in Christ Marquetta and Brigittia my brothers in Christ , Jonathan Harrison and Dale Hairston, thank you both for encouraging me and getting me moving with this book. My work family, Denise, Patricia, Ms. Odessa, Joetta, Ronnie and the entire 4A Joint Replacement Crew, My Lunch Bunch Crew, you ladies and gentlemen are my heart. Thank you all for your continual encouragement, love and support.

Big thanks to my wonderful God-parents, Eric and Debbie Sellers and the whole Filling Station Crew. Eric and Debbie, God brought you into my life to keep me straight, over the years ya'll have done just that, even when I was acting all foolish, your prayers never stopped. I love you two so much because you never judged me; you all just loved on me until God got in there and did His work. Thank you.

I want to thank my pastors, Bishop Lyle and Pastor Deborah Dukes. You two have truly encouraged me through the words you have spoken to me. Teaching and encouraging me to "Do it afraid." Lord knows right about now I'm scared out my skull, but I know through your teachings that I have a God who will never forsake or leave me. You have helped me to strengthen the foundation of Jesus Christ in my life. You've shown me, I am fearfully and wonderfully made in God's own image. I'm happy and so very blessed that God brought me into Harvest. May God continue to bless your ministry, your home, and your entire family! Thank you.

John Medley, my partner and wonderful friend, you have helped calm me down and helped me to remember my smile. Because of you I have learned that just because it's not in the time I want, doesn't mean it won't happen. I'm beyond happy God brought you into my life.

To the many that have read and reviewed this book, I want to say thank you all for your time and your words of encouragement and correction.

Over the years God has brought different people into my life who told me I have a gift that I needed to use. Thank you all for your continuous support and words of encouragement. May God bless all of you with abundance.

Introduction

I've written this book because I know there are so many men and women like me who've been through a lot in life and who are looking for some sunshine through all the clouds hovering over them. I wanted to show that, even though you may be going through something right now, even though you may think you're not worth of anything, you have a Saviour and a Lord who can show you your worth. He can show you how valuable you are in his kingdom. He can save your soul and open your eyes to how beautiful you are in Him. According to Psalms 139:14 we are fearfully and wonderfully made, marvellous are thy works. Marvellous are His works. We are His work so we are absolutely marvellous. We are made in God's image. With Christ in our lives we can become beautiful in every way.

In this book there are passages before each poem. Take your time to read and study them. Find out what our Father truly feels about you.

Stay blessed and encouraged through Christ Jesus.

Table of Contents

Ebony N'Tantala

I will praise thee; for I am fearfully and wonderfully made: marvellous are thy works; and that my soul knoweth right well. My substance was not hid from thee, when I was made in secret, and curiously wrought in the lowest parts of the earth. Thine eyes did see my substance, yet being unperfect; and in thy book all my members were written, which in continuance were fashioned, when as yet there was none of them.

Psalms 139:14-16

Who I Am (A Beautiful Work Of Art)

The day the Lord made me,
He through in a bit of this, a little of that,
With a sprinkle of this, a whole lot of that
Then He Looked at His finished work
And said, "It Is good."

Whoa, I am A Beautiful Work of Art!

He blessed me first with
My beautiful chocolate caramel
Coated complexion

Then with His wonderful artistic hand
He added a light sprinkle of freckles here and
there, just to give me a little flare.
Then My Father gave me
My almond shaped eyes.
Eyes that love to look, watch and see
All the things this world has in store for me.
Now that I think about it-
From the top of my five feet four inch frame
To the very soles, of my pedicure feet...

I am— A Beautiful Work of Art.

From My almond shaped eyes
To the freckles on my face

To the length and curve of my neck,

I am-A Beautiful Work of Art

From my broad shoulder
To my hour glass shape

A beautiful work of art I am

From my thick strong thighs
To my big shapely calves

I am—A beautiful work of art.
From curve and contours of my ankles
To the very tips of my toes,
To the arc at the soles of my feet
An Absolutely beautiful work of art, I AM!

My outer beauty and class
You must understand,
Is an analogous of the beauty
That's found on the inside of me.
Better is He who is in me then
He that is in the world...
See on the inside of me dwelling
Comfortably is my Lord and Savior Christ!

See, He assures my beauty never dies
Continuously reminding me to always,
Respect, love and forgive not only
Myself, but those around me,
Even those who refuse to respect, love or
forgive me.
He has given me,
A couple more beatitudes that I hold dear,
Courage, faith, love, strength and wisdom to
live
Through heartache and pain dealt to me
By those who've claimed to
Love and care for me...
A pin up model I may not be
But a beautiful woman, I am.
Beautiful inside and out.
God-fearing and hardworking,
Mom of three and many more
God has bounded to me.

A world scholar or genius
I may not be

Intelligent I will always be,
Armed with knowledge, acceptance and
understanding
Thoughtfully, given to me from my Father
above.

Rich with wealth I may never have
Fame may never come my way
Rich and privileged with
Family and the love of God I will always be.
I've been given gifts, talents and abilities
That, no one on the earth could
Ever take away
Or even understand...
Self confidence coupled with Inner beauty
sprinkled with strength, courage and wisdom,
Topped off by my love and faith for My God,
Collectively these things make me—

Who I am, A Beautiful Work of Art...

In case you were wondering
What exactly my name means,

It's Black Beautiful Princess.
It's taken me many years to realize
That's exactly who and
What I am and will always be!

Thou therefore endure hardness, as a good soldier of Jesus Christ.
No man that warreth entangleth himself with the affairs of this life; that he may please him who hath chosen him to be a soldier.

2nd Timothy 2:3-4

Black tear Drops

Sometimes my writings are like
Black tear drops on a page,
Crying out the things I hold
Deep in my heart.
Things I'm too ashamed or
Apprehensive to say.

Afraid of what one may think of me
If I were to speak these words.

Sometimes I use my words as a sword stabbing at
the unjust things I see. Wondering if my eyes
should believe the sorrow and the BS they
witness.

Hoping the ones that they pertain to bleed, if not
physically at least mentally, emotionally, leaving
their heart scarred forever, as they have done
to me and others before me.

Sometimes my writings are like black tear drops
stains on a page, confessing my sadness, my
sorrows, my weaknesses....

Confessing my empathy,
My hatred, my fears.

Sometimes my words are like black tear drops
stains on a page,

Telling of the happiness and joy others bring.

Sometimes my writings are like black tear drops
running down the page overjoyed about the

passion, the love, the tenderness others
have brought to me.

If you read my words can you tell what my Black
Tear Drops Mean?

Should he reason with unprofitable talk? Or with speeches wherewith he can do no good?
Job 15:3

JUST CHILL

Not knowing what to say
When things don't go my way
Sometimes I want to shout
"THIS CAN'T BE WHAT LIFE'S ABOUT!!"
Sometimes I'm red hot
Other times I'm not.
Don't ask me what's wrong
Cuz for real;
I'm tired of that song
If I want to talk, then I will
Don't force the issues
Just chill.
If I'm not talking today,
Then maybe tomorrow I will.
But for now...
Go with the flow
Leave me alone
And just chill.

Are not two sparrows sold for a farthing? And one of them shall not fall on the ground without your Father. But the very hairs of your head are all numbered. Fear ye not therefore, ye are of more value than many sparrows.
Matthew 10:29-31

Damaged Goods

Damage goods, Damaged goods
Can't you all see?
Damaged goods, Damaged goods,
So how can _He_ love me?
My internal damage once again defeats me.
Since I'm afraid to give or even show all of me.
My disfigured innards leave much to be desired.
I don't have a mere blemish or a tiny scratch,
No small wound that will heal over. LOL!!!!!
Oh no, not me! I have deep down festering gashes
Filled with angry foul smelling pus,
Overflowing with the diseases;
Of fear and mistrust.
Secondary to hopelessness, and hate,
Related to the BS I've had to go through,
The raping, the beatings, the always leavings.
Damaged goods, Damaged goods
For all to see.
Damaged goods, Damaged goods
So how can _He_ love me?
Fool ya'll with the half smiles,
My, oh so chirper attitude.
My fake optimism holds ya'll over.
My confidence is seen in
Every one of my steps.
I hold my head high, my shoulders back
My chest out, I strut, I pause, I grin.

I've duped not only you but myself
Into believing, that I'm anything but,
The injured, emotionally batter woman
That I've become.
Damaged goods, Damaged goods,
For all to see.
Damaged goods, Damaged goods
How can _He_ love me?
When I can't even, Love myself.

*And God shall wipe away all tears
from their eyes; and there shall be no
more death, neither sorrow, nor crying,
neither shall there be any more pain:
for the former things are passed away.
Revelation 21:4*

Do I want a Husband?

Do I want a husband, hmmm let me think
Heeecckk Naaaww son, are you sick or just plain
crazy?
You really must not know my story.
Let me shine a light for you to get some clarity...
A wife to someone
For what?
To be property,
To be hit on when it's convenient,
To be raped in front of my son
And have him say to this day
"I remember what daddy did to you, mom."
A husband, naw that's not for me.
Been there done that,
Two times as a matter of fact
I have the broken heart and
Broken spirit to prove it.
I refuse to go back again,
To the loss of self,
The love of myself no longer existing
Trying to find a small ray of sunshine
Through so much pain.
I can't say I wish to experience that again.

I can't do it!
I can't be another punching bag!
I can't return to being a second rate citizen!
I can't be treated as a figure of lust, something
For him to just deposit his seed in.
I'm worth more then that, Right?
I have to be worth more than that.
Having him committing, continual adultery
With his precious women;
Gin, Vodka, Brandy, and Mary Jane.
With those chicks I couldn't begin to compete.
Cuz his women weren't flesh like me.
They tended to wrap him
around their little fingers
Wherever they went
He would be more than happy to follow.
Spending countless hours, adoringly, loving
them.
He never wanted to spend time like that with me.
What did they have that I don't?
Why couldn't he find that same love
And interest in me?
God, what's wrong with me?
I'm worth more than them, right?
Having my children not understanding

What they did to make daddy mad at them
why there's so much yelling,
Why is daddy hurting Mommy?
Why? What's going on?
What did mommy do wrong this time?
They deserve more than that, right?
They should have better then that, Right?
They need to know that's not real love, right?
So, right now a marriage, a husband, naw,
Right now, I just can't see.
At this moment, I just want to be me!

Ebony Freeman
Hmph, naw for real, ya'll,

I just want to be FREE...

*Whither shall I go from thy spirit? Or
whither shall I flee from thy presence?
If I ascend up into heaven, thou art
there: if I make my bed in hell, behold,
thou art there.
If I take the wings of the morning,
and dwell in the uttermost parts of the
sea;
even there shall thy hand lead me,
and thy right hand shall hold me.
Psalms 139:7-10*

RUNNING

Awww. Stop!!
PLEASE JUST STOP,
I don't want to hear your word
I didn't ask to be free,
Please God just let me be.
Let me live my life my way
Let me love my way,
Just, let me
Just let me
Run away.

Running
From my past

Running
From my present

Running
From the future that could be

Running
From the lies

Running
From the truth
That, my child, you can no longer do,
The destiny I have for you is waiting.
Lean on me, rest in my arms, find peace.

NOOOO...LET ME BE, I JUST NEED TO RUN
Running,
Trying to get far away from you.

Running
From your voice that continuously calls
Running in circles is what I've been doing

Running away from the help I say I'm needing
Plugging my ears as I make my escape
Sorry Lord, I can't listen to your message today.

Stop running
From my healing love,
Stop running,
My love is everlasting
It will give you the rest and
true love you seek.

Running
From your gentle stroke that calms my heart

Running
From anything or anyone that may mean too much.

Running,
Terrified, of your healing touch.

One thousand nine hundred and seventy-seven
years ago. I shed my blood for you
So you wouldn't have to run.
I Shed MY BLOOD so that today
I could wipe Your tears and fears away with a
word.

NO!!! You don't understand!!
I've been running so hard, for so long
I should be ten times smaller.
Instead, the weight I carry
Has become a silent assassin,
Suffocating, asphyxiating, stifling all of me.
Slowly it has imprisoned, my heart, my spirit, my
soul.

Keeping me hostage; to hurt, pain, anger,
bitterness and rage.
I can't do anything but run.

You can do something other then run
Call my name.
Try it, just once and see.
Call my name.
And MY Spirit will calm and
Set you free

JESUS PLEASE HELP ME!!!

Jesus answered and said unto her,
Whosoever drinketh of this water shall
thirst again:
But whosoever drinketh of the water
that I shall give him shall never thirst;
but the water that I shall give him
shall be in him a well of water
springing up into everlasting life.
John 4:13-14

WOMAN LOST

Bitterness and rage filling my heart and mind
Like pages out of a horror book
Mad at all in which I encounter
Not caring on whose shoes I trample
Angry at myself for changing as much as I have
Continuously, believing, reliving the hurt of my
past
Wanting to be free of all the hurt and pain
Never having to suffer like this again
I, I feel so lost, so alone
Looking for the place, I can call home.
Trying to get the apprehension and strife
Out of my life
Trying to free myself from my bonds
Not knowing to whom I should turn.
Humph, who to trust to show me love, guidance
Who can give me strength that I need to live each
day?
I trust no one cuz no one is there to shield me
From the heartache and pain I face.
To whom can I call, to whom can I turn
When my anger's on overload and
My heart and soul does burn?

The LORD himself goes before you and will be with you; he will never leave you nor forsake you. Do not be afraid; do not be discouraged."
Deuteronomy 31:8 (NIV)

Fantasy vs. **Reality**

My fantasy life would be...
Being the wife of a loving, caring
God fearing, hardworking man;
Who wants to be with me
Just because he loves
The sound of my voice,
The freckles on my face,
The shape and feel of my body
Even when I'm old and gray.

My fantasy man...
Would love me with all he has
Because, in return, he'd know
He'd get the same.
Ounce for ounce,
Bit for bit.

Growing, spiritually, emotionally,
Physically together
Learning to become one
With God and each other.

Humph...
Yeah, that's my fantasy man.

My fantasy man
Loves the shape of my hips
Their swaying could get him excited
Just by him taking a glimpse
Of me walking down the street

My fantasy man
Would want me exclusively;
No other woman could compare
To his caramel, chocolate coated teddy bear.
Humph
Yeah that's my fantasy man.
My fantasy man
Is a man who could be
A father and friend to this family
Made before him.
He's filled with compassion, strength and love Given
to him from the Man above.
There has to be someone
With all these qualities I seek
Cause for real,
No longer will I compromise
My heart, mind, body, nor spirit
To just anyone on the street
That may have one or two
Qualities I seek.

In my fantasies I have a king
Who treats me as his loving queen.
My children are his children,
His children are mine.
Humph....
Yeah, that's my fantasy.
The funny thing about fantasies is;
They're only in my dreams.

The reality of the whole thing is;
My fantasy, at least for now,
Is just that
A Fantasy.
Cause in reality...

I'm a single, hardworking,
God fearing mother of three,
Who has settled one too many times
For less than my king.

For now, my king
Seems to be a figment in
My fantasies
So distant I can't seem to grasp his hand
Let alone his heart.
Humph

That's my reality.

In reality;
Brothers ain't looking for a pre-made family
Helping to raise some other man's children,
Shooooott, that's craziness to most brothers I
meet.

Yeah,
That's my reality.
My reality is going to work
Trying to make the ends meet.
Going to church, trying to find
Who God wants me to be

Then home again
To take care of my children.
My reality is climbing into my bed
At the end of my day
Finding nothing
But my pillows to comfort me.

If only my fantasies
Could intertwine with my reality
Hooonneeeyyy, woooweee
I'd be on top of the world!

But the reality is...
Fantasy, is just that... fantasy.
So, while I sleep
I will dream
Of my fantasy king
Until I open my eyes to my reality.

Yea, the darkness hideth not from thee; but the night shineth as the day: the darkness and the light are both alike to thee.

Psalms 139:12

The Pit

Being hurt time and again
Makes one come to a reality
Quicker and quicker with each passing day
Trying to see good in people I meet

But here lately,
Bad things are all I seem to see.
Then the questions come one by one
The "what ifs", the "how comes"
The "what if I did it this way instead"

I've become afraid to find Happiness
Since Misery only seems to show its wretched
head.

Deeper and deeper I've begun to sink into
A dismal, horrible, smelly pit of despair
As I try to claw my way out
I get knocked back down again and again.
The harder I try, the darker it gets.
The more I climb, the deeper it gets.
The harder I push, the tighter it gets.
The more I scream for help,
The lonelier it gets.

I can feel myself being pulled down
Into the abyss of shadows and gloom,
Silently hoping, crying, pleading
For someone, anyone to pull me out of this,
This tangled web of darkness,
Hopelessness, heartache, heartbreak and
sorrow.

Time and again,
I've tried to climb out, but to no avail.
Each time I've tried to escape from this hole on
my own,
Claws as long as knives grab at me
Pulling, tugging, tormenting, cutting me
Everywhere they touch.

Increasing the screams of terror and anguish that
fester deep within my heart penetrating straight
to my soul.

Please someone help me!
Someone please quiet the voices of hatred

In my head screaming at me to
"shut up, shrivel up and die,
No one will care whether you're here or not"
Quiet the voices of despair
Continuously telling me "you won't make it out
of here alive,
You don't matter enough for anyone to care."

**PLEASE SOMEONE RESCUE ME,
I NO LONGER WANT TO BE TRAPPED IN
THIS PRISON OF DESPONDENCY AND
DESPERATION.
SOMEONE PLEASE FREE ME!!!**

Can anybody hear me?!

"Shhhhh, hush and listen to Me."
Nothing of this world can save you
From this pit of damnation.
No longer can you go by your rules,
You have to stop, take time out for Me
Find out who I am, why I've willingly rushed to
rescue you with My saving love and grace.

"HAHAHAHA, yeah ok and you are…?"

I am the one you've been searching for
But are too blind to ever see
I am the one who comforts you
when you are hurting
I am the voice who's always talking to you
Yet you've closed your ears to my voice.
I am the constant knocking on your heart
You always ignore
Only In My name can you rebuke this demon who
has kept
You imprisoned in your own mind of depression.
My father did not give you the spirit of fear
But of power, and of love, and of a sound mind.
I am who I Am
I am the Lord!

The only ONE who can save you.

Come unto me, all ye that labour and are heavy laden, and I will give you rest. Take my yoke upon you, and learn of me; for I am meek and lowly in heart: and ye shall find rest unto your souls. For my yoke is easy, and my burden is light.
Matthew 11:28-30

Spiritual Baggage

As I kneel down at the alter…
Casting my cares upon you…
I struggle to rise from my knees
Because of the spiritual baggage
I can't seem to relinquish…

What's your spiritual baggage?

Do you feel like the woman at the well…
Been married a time or two
And the one you're with now ain't even yours...
Going from one marriage to the next trying to
Find that perfect connection, that perfect fit.
Trying to quench your unquenchable thirst?

That's your spiritual baggage.

Or maybe you're more like Mary Magdalene,
Giving your soul away, one piece at a time.
Giving a lil piece here, a lil piece there,
Till you don't know where or who you really are.
Every time you decide to
Lay me down with someone new
Who only wants a minute part of you.
You lose something.

What's your Spiritual baggage?

Are you more like Peter?
Forever boasting and running your mouth, yet
When it comes down to showing
Who your Lord and Savior is
You Deny Him for your own sake.

YOU DENY HIM FOR YOUR OWN
SAKE!!!
Humph, now that's some serious, serious
baggage.

Could it be you're emulating Matthew?
Living the high life, partying day and night.
Mr. or Ms. Entertainment.
Taking from those you should be giving to,
Cheating others whenever it pleases you.

Humph what a life,
With so much baggage, what a life.

What's your spiritual baggage?

Are you imitating Noah?
Drinking day in and day out,
Trying to drown out your life's pains and
sorrows,
Looking for your quick fix,
Your redemption in a bottle.

Are your shoulders getting weary,
Constantly carrying the false possessions of your
past?

Have the muscles in your back worn out
From the relentless lugging, pulling and hauling
Of your past and present insecurities?

Have your knees become weak from supporting
The OVERLOAD of baggage
You've placed upon your shoulders?

WELL THEN, PUSH!!
Push past the doubt, push past the pain, push
past all your shame, Push past the lies Satan has
constantly convinced you to claim.
Throw off that baggage place it at the feet
Of the one who can change it all
The one who can fight this battle.
You can't begin to understand
The one who sits on the right hand side of God,
Interceding on your behalf.

Get up, fight, scream, yell, holler, praise ye the
Lord!!!

What you don't seem to comprehend is
Jesus, Wants your baggage, to dispose of it
He wants to wrap you in His robe of
righteousness stained with His blood of salvation,
scented with the Fragrance of God's perfect
mercy, grace, and love.

The baggage you carry doesn't represent who
you are.
The blood of Jesus, says, you are a child of God.
Who has the blessing of Abraham over their life.

Do you have the pass code that changes any
situation?
The code that opens any door, that disposes of all
Spiritual baggage, in your life?
The code which turns that storm of yours into
A beautiful sun shiny day…

J e s u s!!!
All extra baggage welcomed!!!

But the God of all grace, who hath called us unto his eternal glory by Christ Jesus, after that ye have suffered a while, make you perfect, stablish, strengthen, settle you.
1Peter 5:10

<u>MY way</u> of Thinking

YEARNING *FOR WHAT I WANT, BUT MAY NEVER POSSESS*
GUILT *FOR THE THINGS IN MY PAST I CAN NOT CHANGE*
STRESSED *ABOUT EVERY ASPECT OF MY LIFE*
TEMPTED *TO RETURN TO WHAT MAY OR MAY NOT BE MY SECURITY.*
REBELLIOUS *AGAINST THOSE WHO TRY TO RULE OVER ME*
ANXIOUS *ABOUT WHAT THE FUTURE HOLDS*
LEARNING *TO LOVE ME FOR ME*
BEGINNING *TO BE A VIRTUOUS WOMAN*
BELIEVING *THAT GOD CAN AND WILL GET ME THROUGH*
KNOWING *THAT, I CAN DO ALL THINGS THROUGH CHRIST WHO STRENGTHENS ME.*
FINDING *THIS WOMAN GOD HAS CREATED IS BEAUTIFUL AND SMART.*
FREEDOM IS ONLY A PRAISE AWAY.

The steps of a good man are ordered by the LORD: and he delighteth in his way. Though he fall, he shall not be utterly cast down: for the LORD upholdeth him with his hand.

Psalms 37:23-24

Worthy

Humph, you sit and wonder why at
times u see me with my head down
trying real hard not to make eye
contact...
Have u ever wondered why sometimes
my smile doesn't reach my eyes.

It has to do with my past...
No one knows its full extent.
Except for the Lord and myself...

You treat me so nice
You love me so much
But would you feel the same
If I opened myself up?

See my life has been
Somewhat of a struggle
My biological mom, wow...
Yeah well, I never really knew her

Do u know the only memory I have of
her is...
Her "friend" coming over and she
putting my brother, sister and myself

out the house...
And she did all this while
she was still my father's spouse...

She passed when I was young;
I never got to tell her how I felt...

Never got to ask her the questions
Why and how come, and what was
really wrong...
I never got to say good bye or mom,
I'm mad at you but I love you
anyway...
I never got to hug her or to say good-
bye...
As a matter of fact I only recently got
to cry....
I never understood why she never

came back
Why she never called or even wrote...
I never understood why she rejected
the two of us.

Then I think of the pain of violation
From those I should've been able to
trust in...
The husband, who promised to protect

me and made me his wife, comes to
mind. He abused and brought torment
to my life...

Then another promised to respect and
honor me
He did things of disrespect and
dishonor
To my body, mind and my soul...

Do you still wonder?
Can't you see I'm not worthy...
I'm not worthy to look at
Let alone give praise and honor to
Thee...
I'm not worthy to give
You worship
I'm not worthy to give
You praise...

My soul is filled with the filth of my
past...
The avoidable heartaches,
unavoidable pain and
So many unintelligent mistakes.
All of this I just can't seem to get past...

If u look at my heart
You would see;

A little girl trying to be free...
Free from past hurt and pain.
Free from so much sin and shame
Trying to make up the wrong
By trying to do right...

So, when you see my head down
my eyes averted, tears streaming down
my face.
I'm a little girl lost trying to be found.

I want to one day be able to look at
ME,
And say: yeah I know that girl
She's been hurt,
She's had plenty of pain

But she is worthy....

For it is written, I will destroy the wisdom of the wise, and will bring to nothing the understanding of the prudent. Where is the wise? where is the scribe? where is the disputer of this world? hath not God made foolish the wisdom of this world?

1^{*st*} *Corinthians 1:19-20*

…AND THEN I WOKE UP

Eyes closed to the truth
Heart hardened from any love
Running from any peace I may find
I once was a Woman Lost.
The Pit of depression did once

Have a hold on me
Fantasy and Reality did once
Cause me sheer confusion
The fear of a man hurting me,
Having power over me, controlling me, made
me never
To want a husband again.

….And Then, I woke up.
Opening my eyes to the
Love and favor of God's grace and love
Realizing through Him,
I can and will become better.

No longer do I have to be
Trapped in a pit of Depression and despair,
Believing I'm soiled, tainted,
Damaged Goods that
No one could ever love.

He rid me of the Spiritual Baggage
Clogging the closet of my heart,
Overpowering, controlling every aspect of my
life

Not knowing how to find any peace of mind.

I woke up
To Jesus saying...

*give me your heavy
Burdens; you can be free
Of this unnecessary weight you bear.*

NO longer will the Black Tear Drops
On my pages scream rage
Unless it's against those
Who war against my Lord and Savior.

No longer
Do I run away from God's precious love
Now, humbly I embrace it,
Cherishing His perfect Love,
Happily Running to His open arms Whenever
I get the chance.

So now, I Just Chill...

Giving control of my life over to my
Lord and Savior Jesus Christ.
Relishing in the fact that I am
Worthy of His undying love

See, my way of thinking is;
If He loved me enough to die for me, maybe
Him being in control of my life
Will actually save me
From me.

Lord, I thank you
for continually waking me up.
Until my eyes opened

And I finally woke up.

Be careful for nothing; but in every thing by prayer and supplication with thanksgiving let your requests be made known unto God.
And the peace of God, which passeth all understanding, shall keep your hearts and minds through Christ Jesus.
Philippians 4:6-7

Lord, my prayer to You

Lord,
There are so many things on my heart I don't
Know exactly where or even how to start...
Lord, I ask you to open my eyes to your will
Open my ears to hear your words for my life
Let my tongue say the things
You wish it to say.
Let it speak only words that are acceptable to
you
Father, let my heart be light
And my eyes be bright
Continuously stayed on you and your love.
Open me to what ever your will may be.
Letting me see clearly when the sun is shining
Or when the rain is blinding my sight.
Heavenly Father,
Your vessel, I truly want to be
Living for you as you live through me
Is the desire and longing of my heart.
I want to be the sanctified, virtuous woman
You have called me to be.
Let others see how great and wonderful you
are
Through the gifts, talents and abilities
You have generously bestowed upon me
Let the sanctification you've bestowed upon
me

Encourage my children to call on you.
In their times of happiness and joy
As well as their times of need and sorrow.
Let the anointing you pour upon me
Be a blessing unto you and the
Many others you've placed in my path.
Lord, let my light shine for you and you alone
Let me continue to seek you and your face
In all my situations, whether joyous or sad.

May praises forever flow from my lips to your
ears.
In Jesus' name I pray, Amen.

For the LORD God is a sun and shield: the LORD will give grace and glory: no good thing will he withhold from them that walk uprightly.
O LORD of hosts, blessed is the man that trusteth in thee.
Psalms 84:11-12

LEARNING TO BLOOM AGAIN

I once heard a wise woman say:
"One thing I can say about a Rose is,
As long as it has its roots,
It will always bloom.
There's a time for it to lay dormant
and
A time for it to flourish."

There have been times in my life
When I have bloomed with an
abundance of petals,
Giving off a beautiful fragrance of
Happiness, well being and
contentment.

Then there have been times
When I have lain dormant
With my thorns visible
to those around me
Ready and more than
Willing to draw blood
From those who got too close.

I'm beginning again.
I'm learning again.

I'm taking the time to learn
Who Ebony N'Tantala, really is.
I'm learning to love myself again.
I'm learning to believe in myself again.

I'm taking the time to ask myself
"Who are you and what do you believe
in?"

I'm learning to bloom again.

I'm taking the time to stop and
Actually hear what people are telling
me.
Not just listening, but hearing their
words.
The positive words I let flow over me
like healing waters helping me
In my emotional journey to recovery.

I am learning to bloom again.

The negative words and things in my
life
I dissect pull them apart, searching
for something
In them that may be there to help me
grow,
Bloom and love once again.
The rest I discard, throw away, forget
about.
See, I don't need nothing,
or nobody holding
Me back from my blooming process.
Because, as you can see,
I am learning to bloom again.
God has shown me He has a knack,
for taking
The negative things in my life, turning
them around
To make the most wonderfully
positive things.

And still I'm learning to bloom.

In my learning I've realized,
I'm flawed; I'm emotionally damaged,

Very headstrong and at times controlling.
I've also learned that I'm strong and Beautiful.
I am fascinating, loving, caring.
Willing to try, willing to learn,
Willing to do what it takes in order for my aromatic

Fragrance of well being and happiness to be inhaled near and far.
As my heart heals,
My once weak stem becomes strong.
As I shake off the snow of mistrust from around my life,
New buds begin to show.
As I love, and am loved,
My petals, which have lain dormant for So long on this rose, have begun to bloom again.

Thank you, Mother Poindexter, for giving me words, of encouragement and wisdom.

*And he took the damsel by the hand,
and said unto her, Talitha cumi; which
is, being interpreted, Damsel, I say
unto thee, arise.*
Mark 5:41

Talitha Cumi

"Talitha Cumi, damsel I say unto thee arise"
Arise out of your sorrow;
Arise out of your pain,
Arise out of your bondage of shame.
Look to the Rabboni, Jesus,
And begin to live again.
"Talitha cumi,
Damsel I say unto thee arise."
What once was your past,
Is no longer your future.
As I called upon Him, screaming;
Rabboni, Master,
Heal me, teach me, free me, fill me,
Make me whole;
Show me how to live and
Love righteously through you.
Hearing the desperation in my voice
He replied:

Cumi,
Arise out of the darkness,
That has had you bound with chains
Of fear for so long.
Cumi,
Arise out of the ashes of your long
held shame.
Your past is dead, the old you is no
more.
Simply arise and stand
Upon My Word and My name
To free you from the bonds and chains
of your past humiliations.

As my tears wash away
My ash covered face,
His blood washed away the stench of
death
That was once my sins.
Jesus healed the scars left upon my
heart, He healed the soreness within
my soul from The Unspeakable pains
of my past.

As I place my hand in His,
I see, it *IS*
Through Him I can still stand,
Through Him, I can still press on,
Through Him, I HAVE RISEN!!!
Risen over my trials and tribulations,
I've risen over my doubts and fears.
I've begun to live and love because:
Greater is He, who is within me,
Than he who is in the world.
Because of Him, I WILL LIVE!!
I am not dead, I am alive. I have
risen!!
Because of Him I am NOW free!!!
"Talithas Cumi, Damsels I say unto
thee arise!!!!!"

A Change is a coming! Can you see it?
I can feel it deep down in my bones,
Straight to my spirit man!

Oh a Change is a Coming just you wait
and see!!!
Watch as the Change overtakes me!!

Acquaint now thyself with him, and be at peace: thereby good shall come unto thee.
Job 22:21

INDEPENDENTLY DEPENDENT

I'm independently dependent on You Lord
Thankful for the very breath You breathe into
me each morning, blessing me to see yet another
day,

I've become dependent.

As I stretch out my limbs and open my eyes, You
bless me with mobility, strength and sight
Every second of every day.

Lord, how I've become dependent …

Spending time with you sends
Me on a supernatural high
That no one could ever comprehend
Unless, they too,
Are independently dependent on You.

As You minister to my spirit.
With encouragement, protection, correction and
healing.

As I bask in the glow of Your awesomeness,
I begin to praise, worship and glorify You.
Lifting Your mighty name on high.

Independently I call on You,
Independently I praise only Your name
Independently I fall to my knees to glorify You as
I enter into Your presence.

I can't follow the crowd
I can't wait 'til,
It's the fashionable thing to do.
I'm not waiting on Jordan, Jessica or Jill.

**I HAVE TO BE INDEPENDENT.
I GOTTA BE INDEPENDENTLY
DEPENDENT ON YOU AND ONLY YOU.**

You are my air, my strength, my knowledge.

YOU ARE MY ALL.

So I must be dependent on you.
To give me the rhema word I need
To fulfill your will for my life.
So I bow to you, humbly giving myself
Over to your will because I've become
Independently dependent only on you Jesus.

Favour is deceitful, and beauty is vain:
but a woman that feareth the LORD,
she shall be praised.
Give her of the fruit of her hands;
and let her own works praise her in the
gates.
Proverbs 31:30-31

Virtuous Woman

Whoso loveth instruction, loveth
knowledge: Who can find a virtuous
Woman?

Her price is far above rubies....

The Word is her instruction manual
Guiding her through life's ups and downs
Presenting her with the meaning of true,
unconditional love showing her where true
happiness can be found.

The Lord is her one and only master
Prayer is her reflection, her escape, her
passion,
Her way of worshipping the One
Who's blessed her with great abundance.

Her mistakes, trials and tribulation, are her
stepping stones, her teaching tools, in
becoming who God wants her to be.
Fear is not a companion to her,
Because she is made in The Father's image.

Who can find a virtuous woman?
Not wavering in her faith that
Her love for God will accentuate the
Love for her husband.

<ins>Only with God as the crown upon her husband's head,</ins>
<ins>Can she be the jewel upon his arm,</ins>
<ins>The other half that makes him complete.</ins>

A virtuous woman is a jewel to her husband;
The bone that helps to hold him up.
She is the rib from Adam
Walking by her husband's side encouraging,
Helping, guiding, submitting, respecting.
The one who God has brought into her life,
To help guide, respect and encourage her.
What God has brought together may no man,
Woman, or beast put asunder.

Who can find a virtuous woman?
She is a light to her children.
She raises her children in the way of the Lord.

Praying, correcting, loving, teaching,
keeping them in the way God would have her to do.

Who can find a virtuous woman?
Her price is far above rubies...
Proverbs 31:10 a virtuous woman

And all these blessings shall come on thee, and overtake thee, if thou shalt hearken unto the voice of the LORD thy God. Blessed shalt thou be in the city, and blessed shalt thou be in the field. Blessed shall be the fruit of thy body, and the fruit of thy ground, and the fruit of thy cattle, the increase of thy kine, and the flocks of thy sheep.

Deuteronomy 28:2-4

BLESSINGS

BLESSING, BLESSINGS BLESSINGS
ALL AROUND THAT'S ALL I CAN SEE,
IS HOW YOU CONTINUE TO
BLESS AND FAVOR ME.
WHAT, CAN'T YOU ALL SEE IT
THE SPRING I HAVE IN MY STEP
THE SMILE PLANTED ON MY FACE
THE WAY I SING PRAISES TO GOD'S
NAME
BLESSINGS, BLESSINGS BLESSINGS
ALL AROUND
THAT'S ALL I CAN SEE
I CHERISH THE CONTINUED
BLESSING AND FAVOR
YOU GIVE TO ME!

YOU'VE GIVEN ME BACK THE YEARS
I'VE LOST WITH MY SISTER AND MY
BROTHER THE TWO THAT COME FROM
MY BIOLOGICAL MOTHER
I'M OFFICIALLY NO LONGER THE
ELDEST,
I NOW HAVE ONE
WHO'S OLDER THAN ME.
HALLEUAH PRAISES TO YOUR NAME
JESUS!

BLESSINGS, BLESSINGS BLESSINGS
ALL AROUND
THAT'S ALL I CAN SEE
I GLORIFY YOU FOR SUCH AN AWESOME
BLESSING!
LORD MY BROTHER YOU'VE GIVEN
BACK
HAS BEEN SENT TO PROTECT THAT
RIGHTS OF THOSE WHO CAN'T PROTECT
THEMSELVES LORD,
I HAVEN'T HAD A CHANCE TO MEET
HIM FACE TO FACE
I ASK YOU TO WATCH OVER AND
PROTECT HIM. BRING HIM HOME SAFE,
WITH A SPRING IN HIS STEP AND A
PRAISE ON HIS LIPS FOR YOU...
BLESSINGS, BLESSINGS
BLESSING ALL AROUND THAT'S ALL I
CAN SEE
I PRAISE YOU FOR EACH AND EVERY
BLESSING.
THANK YOU FOR FOUR MORE NEPHEWS,
AND ANOTHER BEAUTIFUL NIECE.
LORD, I PRAISE YOU FOR MY OLDER
SISTER,
I CAN'T BELIEVE SHE ACTUALLY LOOKS
A BIT LIKE ME. AT LEAST WE DO IF YOU
LOOK AT OUR EYES

LORD, THE WORLD HAS TAKEN MORE
THEN THIRTY YEARS FROM US
BUT I KNOW YOU CAN AND WILL
RESTORE EACH AND EVERY ONE.
BLESSINGS, BLESSINGS BLESSINGS
ALL AROUND, THAT'S ALL I CAN SEE ALL
BECAUSE ONE DAY I DECIDE TO FOLLOW
THEE
YEARS AND YEARS I HAD PRAYED
NEVER THINKING
I WOULD ONE DAY SEE THEIR FACES OR
HEAR THEIR VOICES.

THEN ONE NIGHT YOU TOLD ME TO
FORGIVE THOSE WHO I'VE HELD
CAPTIVE FOR SO LONG   THEN
"BAM" JUST LIKE THAT
THE FOLLOWING DAY SHE FOUND ME!!!

WHOEVER THOUGHT FACEBOOK COULD
ACTUALLY CHANGE MY LIFE.

HALLEUAH, THANK YOU JESUS!!!

BLESSINGS, BLESSINGS
BLESSING ALL AROUND, THAT'S ALL I
CAN SEE.
I'M HONORED IN HOW YOU CONTINUE
TO BLESS AND FAVOR ME.

Whosoever therefore shall confess me before men, him will I confess also before my Father which is in heaven. But whosoever shall deny me before men, him will I also deny before my Father which is in heaven.
Matthew 10:32-33

I AM ONE

I am one
Who sits and tries to figure out what
the day will bring

I am one
Who cries when they don't know
what else to do.
I am one
Who prays when all else has failed.
I am one.

I am one,

Who wishes to please.
Yet at times I feel
I never please enough
or please

Everyone I should.

I am one
Who's figured out that...
Being happy begins with loving and
Believing in the one true God.
I am one.

I am one
Who will not settle for less then the
best in my life.
I am one
Who has learned that the BEST

Is what the Lord can and will give
me.

I am one
Who remembers why Christ died for
me
And for all those who surround me.

I am one
Who's not afraid to say that God
Is the way, the truth, and the life.
That Jesus IS my Lord and Saviour
I am one.

Am I the only one,
Who can admit to her faults,
The things that need to be worked
on?
Am I the only one,
Who can admit when her light
Has begun to flicker and is in danger
of
Being smothered out completely?

I am damaged goods, but I've found
that
He can love me even if I am damaged
He and only He can make me whole
again.

I am one
Among many damaged spirits and
souls,
That Satan had convinced they would
never make it.
I am one
Of many who's yelled, "Devil you are
a liar."

I am one
Who's saved by the blood of Jesus
Christ.

I am one
Who is loved by the Most High God.
I am one.

Then he said unto them, Go your way, eat the fat, and drink the sweet, and send portions unto them for whom nothing is prepared: for this day is holy unto our LORD: neither be ye sorry; for the joy of the LORD is your strength.
Nehemiah 8:10

THE JOYS IN LIFE

TODAY I STAND HERE PROUDLY
PROCLAIMING AND
PRAISING HIM FOR HE IS THE GOD OF
THE FIFTY MILLION, TWO HUNDRED
THOUSAND, NINTY-FOURTH CHANCE…
HE'S GIVEN ME THIS TEMPLE TO
CONSTANTLY PRAISE AND GLORIFY HIM.

Time and again I have failed,
Yet, He still loves me and guides me.
He's never given up on me,
That's what brings joy to my life

The joys in my life,
Are not the things I can
See, they're the things I can stand up and say
"Thank You Lord for bringing me through."
My tongue can not sing enough praises
Unto you for all the love You've given me!

I'M BLESSED!
I'M LOVED!
I'M CHERISHED!
BY THE ONE TRUE GOD!
BY MY FAMILY!
BY MY FRIENDS!

HE'S GIVEN ME THIS TEMPLE TO
CONSTANTLY PRAISE AND GLORIFY HIM

Time and again I have failed,
Yet, he still loves me and guides me.
He's never given up on me.
That's what brings joy to my life
The pains of life are sometimes easier to
remember
I've beaten myself up time and again for my
failures.
I've criticize myself for the handling of my past.
I've let the things I cannot change ruin my life.
Holding myself hostage to my guilt and shame.
I'm still learning to forgive myself,
For past mistakes and actions
That have made my life what it is today.

I'm not perfect; I'm definitely
Not worthy to receive
The abundance of love God
Continuously rains down on me
I've done so much in my life
Not to be forgiven for.
And yet, Jesus has stood by my side,
Carrying me through
My Constant misery, doubt, trouble,
Trials and tribulations.

He's balanced me through my slips,
Slides and stumbles in life
Lovingly; He anchored and saved my soul
When it was hell bound.

HE HAS GIVEN ME THIS TEMPLE TO CONSTANTLY PRAISE AND GLORIFY HIM.

Time and again I have failed
Yet, he still loves me and guides me.
He's never given up on me.
That's what brings joy to my life!

Jesus held me when there
Was no love for me to see.
His ears have always been open
For me to speak and seek Him.
He's been my constant friend,

Never letting me forget
That it is because of His love,
That even my pains can
Turn into the joys in my life.

Seek ye first the kingdom of God and all His righteous and all these things shall be added unto you.
Matthew 6:33

Seek ye First

All what things Lord?
Peace;
You want peace Seek Me First
Joy;
Joy, that'll come in the morning,
But you First have to seek Me.
Strength;
Real strength isn't physical,
It's My Spiritual strength poured into you
To keep you strong and faithful, to help keep you
going.
Happiness;
Happiness is knowing;
I will never leave you
Nor will I forsake you.

Love;
Ask MY Son into your heart and
You will find Love everlasting.
Prosperity;
Prosperity comes from blessing MY kingdom,
When you bless me, I bless you more abundantly.
Seek ye first MY kingdom
Seek ye first MY righteousness,
Seek ye first MY face

And all the peace, joy, strength, happiness, love, and prosperity
Will fall upon you.
But you have to first seek first MY kingdom.

We love him, because he first loved us.
1 John 4:19

When did I Fall?

Falling in love with Jesus,
Falling in love with Jesus,
Falling in love with Jesus
Was the best thing I ever, ever done.

When did I fall?

I fell the day I heard your voice say...

Open your mouth and speak,
The words you feel in your heart
Open your heart and feel—
Emotions locked away,
For your supposed "rainy day"

Open your eyes and see—
The mountains you've climbed and conquered,
The storms, you've been in and survived,
The trials and tribulations,
That have beaten you down
And yet, you've conquered them, you've
overcome,
You're still standing strong as the tower I have
made you.

Or maybe it was the day
You said...

Show me your heart,
I will protect it.

Show me your love
I will nourish it.

Show me your fears
I will defeat them.

I know who you are,
And I love you for it.
Open up and show me,
And I'll give you happiness for eternity.

In His arms I feel protected!
In His arms never disconnected!
In His arms I feel protected!
There's no place I'd rather, rather be.

I fell the day my eyes opened,
To what my heart was feeling...

I fell the day my heart began to listen
To the chorus You were singing.

I fell the day I shut my mouth,
Opened my ears to the masterful
Serenade You were performing.

Reluctantly, my hips began to sway to the undulating beats and rhythms You happily supplied with an Artisan's Perfection. Unwillingly, my head rolled back, my eyes closed and with my mind full of You, I began to drift, miles, and miles away from my troubles and pain.

My hands lifted in praise, not helping, but to worship and honor Your Holy Name.

I believe I fell...
The day, the tears running down
<u>My</u> face,
no longer meant I was hurting,
Rather, they represented the cleansing of my spirit, the renewing of my mind the beginning of my joy.

Maybe, I fell the day I heard Your voice say...

It's ok let it out, CRY,
For your tears of sorrow today shall turn into to shouts of joy tomorrow.
With Me, there is NOTHING to fear.
Open to Me and I'll give you happiness NOT just for today, but for all eternity!

Falling in love with Jesus,
Falling in love with Jesus,
Falling in love with Jesus ,
Is the best thing I've ever, ever done!

That's When I fell In Love with You..

For God so loved the world, that
He gave His only begotten Son,
that whosoever believeth
in Him should not perish, but
have everlasting life

John 3:16

Because of Your Love

Because of Your love
I am growing.
I've grown from a fearful woman, who
Never wanted to try anything new,
Hiding behind my defeats, constantly licking my
scars, critically infecting my own wounds.

Because of Your love,
I can stand,
On my once shaky sea legs,
Rubbery, with a constant fear of failure.

Because of Your love,
I laugh.
I laugh with a real joy
Not the counterfeit giggles
Everyone's grown accustomed to.

Because of Your love,
I smile.
With a twinkle in my eye and joy in my heart
I'm learning, to really smile

Because of Your love,
I give
Of myself freely, not asking for anything
In return; just giving to see
The smiles appear upon other's faces.

Because of Your love,
I care.
Not just for myself,
But for those who can't or won't care for me or
themselves.

Because of Your love,
I'm changing.
No longer do I bear the fruits of
A depressed woman with nowhere to turn.
Now, when you pass me by,
You can smell the distinct
Fragrance of self love,
With a hint of ambition and confidence.

Because of Your love,
I'm learning to love,
Me for who I am, mistakes and all.

Because of Your love,
I'm learning to trust,
In Your word and Your will for my life.
Because of Your love,
I wake up happy each and every day.

Because of Your love,
I've begun to live again.
I've started to see life
The way You wish for me to see it

Because of Your love,
I am free, so very free
Out of the bondage that once held onto me.

Thank You for Your love
Thank You Jesus, for freeing me.

Do you not know that your bodies are temples of the Holy Spirit, who is in you, whom you have received from God? You are not your own; you were bought at a price. Therefore honor God with your bodies.
1 Corinthians 6:19-20

WOMAN FOUND

In a short time I have grown

From doubt, fear and worry

To confidence and inner glory.

No man, woman, boy or girl

Can make me feel pity for what or

Who I am.

No one will make me hurt for ridiculous reasons.

No one will pile false guilt upon me and my life.

No one will make me feel

I haven't grown.

When I know, God has brought

Me a mighty long way.

So, your hurtful words,

Go ahead say them.

A few tears I may cry

My feelings may hurt for a moment

But that won't change the fact

That because of the saving blood of Jesus,

I am now, a Woman found.

I know thy works, that thou art neither cold nor hot: I would thou wert cold or hot. So then because thou art lukewarm, and neither cold nor hot, I will spew thee out of my mouth.

Revelation 3:15-16

Fence Rida

This is for those folks, who think I'm crazy for
Loving God the way I do.

Being the Jesus Freak that I am.
No longer riding the fence between doing
what's Godly and what's worldly,
Being luke-warm to please
Ya'll of this world who only need Jesus as your
Savior...

As for me, personally....
I can't only have Christ as my Savior,
Just calling on Him to get me out of
yet another jam,
I'VE gotten myself into.
Constantly asking for forgiveness for things I
know I shouldn't be doing, cuz I know He'll
give it to me. Conveniently forgetting I have to
reap all that I've sown.
My seeds have to be that of a Harvest worthy
of God above.

I HAVE to have HIM as my
Lord as well as my Savior,
That's the only way it makes sense to me.
I need Him to guide me to where
He needs me to be
I need Him to shift me where
He needs to shift me.
I ain't saying I'm perfect,
nope never will be.

But I AM souled out to Christ and
Christ alone

No longer can I be Fence Rida!

But God hath chosen the foolish things of the world to confound the wise; and God hath chosen the weak things of the world to confound the things which are mighty; And base things of the world, and things which are despised, hath God chosen, yea, and things which are not, to bring to nought things that are: That no flesh should glory in his presence. But of him are ye in Christ Jesus, who of God is made unto us wisdom, and righteousness, and sanctification, and redemption: That, according as it is written, He that glorieth, let him glory in the Lord.

1Corinthians 1:27-31

POLITICALY INCORRECT

Why is it politically correct, for me to
vote for someone
Because of their party they're in What
if the words they're spouting,
Make the entire nation loose
Yet, I'm expected to vote for them
Whether their in majority or rather
the minority.

Why is it politically incorrect,
For me to choose not to vote for
Either of the representing parties
But to write Christ in as my
Candidate of choice.

I, all of the sudden don't love my
Race or my country because I
Don't see anything spectacular
About two men who will
Eventually follow the world Instead of
the Word of the Lord.

Why is it politically correct for me to salute a general,
Clap for the President,
Bow low for kings and queens,
Give honor to those who achieve greatness in this world,
Celebrate those who have been blessed to have yet another year upon this earth...
Yet, folks Cross their arms and get upset

When God says to give
DOUBLE honor to our
Pastors, because they watch for our soul.
You barely want to watch over your own soul, yet these men and women watch over every soul that comes their way, and you have nerve to say;
"their just man I'm not honoring them"
Hmph, Oook

But let Jay-z or Beyonce walk on stage
let's see how quick you jump Up to
honor them.
Screaming clapping, jumping around
for them to
"Hopefully" see you.

Just Pitiful...

Why Can an ATM machine be in a
Club, idly standing by for you to
Eagerly withdraw your hard Earned
money to pay for alcohol That's slowly
but surely destroying Not only your
body but your soul as well.

Now, let a house of God put in an
ATM, for those of us who forget to stop
at the bank on our way to

church, or those who forget their checkbooks...
And all of the sudden the church is greedy...

Don't get it twisted, sweetheart...
It's time for you to get a clue...
The church wants to save your soul;
The club is trying to destroy it.

Why is it ok for the bill collector's to get the money owed to them from your debt, Yet, the money that God deserves you withhold Because in your mind ten percent is too much, for you to give as a thank you for the job that God has provided for you.
Why is it ok for you to pay to see Usher or Mary J.
But you wanna balk you when you have to pay to see Kirk Franklin or Cee Cee & Bee Bee. Can somebody help me to understand please!

And why is it ok for homosexuals to
come out of the closet and be proud of
their "Lifestyle"...
And folks spout;
"Go head honey be you"
Yet, when I come out of the closet
Letting the world know I am a Jesus
Freak and yes my brother, My sister, I
love you but according to God's Word
you're Out of order and wrong,
Folks yell; "don't push your beliefs on
us,
You think you're better than us
Umm....Actually no,
Trust me baby, not better;
I'm just saved, forgiven, loved and I
KNOW who I am in Him.

When did wrong become right and
Right become wrong...

If being politically correct means I
have to give up,
My morals; faith and the love
I have for my Lord and Savior Jesus
Christ...

Then from this time forward,
Till death do I part,
Politically incorrect, I will be.

My soul needs to get and Stay in
God's presences.
The world searched for me to destroy
my soul.
God called on me to save my soul.
And you all wonder why,
I choose to be politically incorrect.

Hast thou not known? Hast thou not heard that the everlasting God, the LORD, the Creator of the ends of the earth, fainteth not, neither is weary? There is no searching of his understanding.

He giveth power to the faint; and to them that have no might, he increaseth strength.

Even the youths shall faint and be weary, and the young men shall utterly fall:

But they that wait upon the LORD shall renew their strength; they shall mount up with wings as eagles; they shall run, and not be weary; and they shall walk, and not faint.

Isaiah 40:28-31

THE JOURNEY

THE JOURNEYS WE TAKE IN LIFE TAKE US DOWN DIFFERENT ROADS... SOME ROADS ARE STRAIGHT AND NARROW, NEVER GIVING US ANY KIND OF TROUBLE. ON THIS ROAD WE NEVER SEE A BUMP, A ROCK, OR A POTHOLE. IT'S JUST SMOOTH SAILING. THESE ARE THE ROADS OR PATHS THAT GOD WISHES US TO BE ON. A ROAD THAT'S STRAIGHT AND NARROW, NEVER FALTERING IN ANY KIND OF WAY, JUST BASKING IN THE GLOW AND THE LOVE OF GOD, GIVING HIM CONTINUAL PRAISE.

MMMMM SOUNDS SO NICE, SO WONDERFUL.

THEN, WE HAVE ROADS THAT BEGIN AND END IN THE SAME EXACT PLACE. BEING AFRAID TO MOVE TOO FAR AWAY FROM YOUR CENTER, FEARING THE UNKNOWN, NEVER WANTING TO TRY TO USE THE GIFTS, TALENTS AND ABILITIES GOD HAS GIVEN YOU, SHRINKING AWAY IN FEAR OF FAILING. THIS IS THE EASY ROAD, FOR THOSE WHO WISH TO LIVE THEIR LIFE IN A BUBBLE. MISTAKES CAN'T BE MADE, AND IF THEY ARE, FIX THEM RIGHT AWAY BEFORE SOMEONE SEES THE BLEMISHES YOU HAVE. THESE ROADS

ARE WORN AND WELL TRAVELED, BECAUSE THEY GO NO PLACE; LEAD NOWHERE.

I ASK MYSELF, WHAT IF I TOOK THE EASY ROAD AND ABORTED MY CHILDREN? MY LIFE WOULD DEFINITELY BE MORE CAREFREE, LESS WORRIES, MORE MONEY TO SPEND, MORE TIME FOR ME. HMPH, YEAH WHAT IF...

WHAT IF I TOOK THE EASY ROAD AND NEVER DIVORCED MY FIRST HUSBAND? HMPH, HAD LIFE IN THE PALM OF MY HAND. NO WORKING FOR ME, NO WAY, A STAY AT HOME MOM, TAKING CARE OF MY CHILDREN.

YEAH, WHAT IF...

WHAT IF I STAYED WITH MY SECOND HUSBAND? HAD A HOUSE, A NICE CAR, HAD ANY AND EVERYTHING I NEEDED...EXCEPT...RESPECT AND LOVE...YEAH WHAT IF...

MAKING A RIGHT OFF THE ROAD OF CHILDLESSNESS, ONTO THE BOULEVARD OF POSSIBLE DEATH, THEN A LEFT ONTO LOW SELF ESTEEM DRIVE.

THAT IS MY ANSWER TO MY "WHAT IFS."

IF I HADN'T HAD MY CHILDREN, I WOULD NEVER KNOW HOW ONE PERSON CAN CHANGE ANOTHER'S LIFE SO

DRAMATICALLY. I WOULD NOT KNOW HOW MUCH I COULD LOVE SOMEONE SO MUCH, JUST BECAUSE. I WOULD NOT KNOW HOW STRONG A LITTLE ONE CAN BE. I WOULD NOT HAVE THE PLEASURE OF WATCHING THEM AS THEY LEARN AND GROW, BECOMING WHO THEY ARE AND WHO THEY WANT TO BE.

IF I HADN'T DIVORCED HUBBY NUMBER 1, I MAY NOT HAVE LIVED TO SEE MY CHILDREN GROW TO WHO THEY ARE TODAY. MY SELF-ESTEEM WOULD HAVE CONTINUED TO PLUMMET EACH DAY UNTIL I BECAME A SHELL OF MY THEN FORMER SELF.

HMPH....

WITH THE LATER HUBBY, WELL, MY SON PROBABLY WOULD THINK IT'S OK TO DRINK LIQUOR ALL DAY AND SMOKE WEED, WHEN YOU HAVE MOUTHS TO FEED AND BILLS TO PAY. HE MAY HAVE COME TO THE CONCLUSION THAT, IN MARRIAGE, THERE IS NO SUCH THING AS RAPE. IF YOU WANT IT, TAKE WHAT YOU WANT. AFTER ALL, SHE IS YOUR WIFE.

MY DAUGHTERS' WOULD HAVE THOUGHT THEIR LIVES WERE WORTHLESS; THAT IT'S JUST THE WAY THINGS ARE SUPPOSED TO BE. CONTINUOUSLY LETTING OTHERS TREAT

YOU LIKE A SECOND-CLASS CITIZEN. ACCEPTING THE MISTREATMENT, THAT CAUSES LOW SELF-ESTEEM, GUILT, AND SHAME.

SOME OF THE JOURNEY'S I'VE TAKEN IN MY LIFE HAVE BEEN HARD AND SOME HAVE BEEN ILL FOUNDED, NOT FULLY THOUGHT THROUGH, YET IN EACH ONE OF THEM I HAVE LEARNED SOMETHING NEW.

I'VE LEARNED AND RELEARNED, TIME AND AGAIN THAT I'M STRONG AND INTELLIGENT. I'M WONDERFUL AND SOMETIMES WISE. I'M JUST LEARNING THAT I AM FEARFULLY AND WONDERFULLY MADE BY MY FATHER ABOVE. I MAY NOT BE ALL THAT I WANNA BE, BUT I KNOW WITH GOD AS MY CAPTAIN, GUIDING MY SHIP, I WILL MAKE IT TO WHERE HE NEEDS ME TO BE.

I'VE LEARNED THAT STRENGTH IS NOT JUST THAT EVERY DAY PHYSICAL FORCE USED IN PICKING THINGS UP. NO, IT'S A MENTAL AND SPIRITUAL FORCE GIVEN TO YOU BY GOD. IF YOU DON'T HAVE THE MENTAL AND THE SPIRITUAL, THEN THE PHYSICAL TRULY DOESN'T MATTER.

THE JOURNEYS I HAVE TAKEN THROUGH THE YEARS HAVE BEEN FILLED WITH POTHOLES, BROKEN CEMENT, FALLEN

TREES, AND A HECK OF A LOT OF OTHER DEBRIS. AT TIMES I'VE FELT LIKE EVERYTHING AROUND ME WAS IN SHAMBLES AND I COULDN'T GO ON. I GOT TIRED OF TRIPPING OVER THE BROKEN GLASS OF EMOTIONS THAT RUN DEEP WITHIN ME. I'VE LEARNED THAT SOMETIME YOU HAVE TO BE CUT BY THE BROKEN SPIRITUAL GLASS TO SEE THAT YOU STILL BLEED; YOU STILL HAVE FEELINGS, EVEN WHEN YOU THINK THAT YOUR MIND, BODY AND SOUL ARE PARALYZED FROM ANY EMOTIONAL ATTACHMENTS.

I MAY HAVE SOME BRUISES, A FEW SCARS, A TAD BIT OF RESIDUAL PAIN, A BIT OF UNEASE HERE AND THERE, A SMIDGEN OF CALCIFICATION AROUND MY HEART AND MAYBE A LITTLE HARDENING OF MY EMOTIONS.

YET, I YELL:

I AM BLESSED, TO WHOEVER WILL LISTEN.

SINCE I TOOK THAT FIRST STEP TO RUN BACK TO MY FIRST LOVE, JESUS CHRIST, I'VE BEEN AWAKENED TO THE STRONG, INDEPENDENT, WONDERFULLY AWESOME WOMAN

I AM.
SO, WHATEVER JOURNEYS YOU MAY
TAKE IN YOUR LIFE, FINDING JESUS,
SEEKING HIS FACE AND HIS WILL FOR
YOUR LIFE WILL CHANGE YOU FOREVER,
FOR THE BETTER. GIVE HIM A TRY!
WHAT'S THAT SAYING; "NOTHING
VENTURED, NOTHING GAINED."
WOULDN'T YOU LIKE TO GAIN A BETTER
RESPECT FOR WHO YOU ARE, WHILE
ACQUIRING KNOWLEDGE OF YOURSELF
AND THE PLAN GOD HAS FOR YOUR LIFE?
WELL, VENTURE OUT! START A NEW
JOURNEY, ONE WITH CHRIST IN
CONTROL!!

BE BLESSED!!!

As many as I love, I rebuke and chasten: be zealous therefore, and repent. Behold, I stand at the door, and knock: if any man hear my voice, and open the door, I will come in to him, and will sup with him, and he with me.

Revelation 3:19-20

THIS SINNERS PRAYER

Heavenly Father, I ask You to forgive me of my sins. The things You can't look upon, the things that have hurt not only me but all those around me. Forgive my selfishness, my anger, my bitterness. Anything I may have done or said that was not pleasing to Your ears or your sight, I ask You to please forgive me.

*Sometimes it seems no matter
What I do, I can't get it right
I'm still doing so many things wrong
At least that's the way I see it.*

*Forgive me for not fully trusting in
You or Your word.*

*Forgive me, for trying to be
My own author and finisher.*

*You know my heart and my mind
And at times they seem to have conflict
My heart wants to live by Your Word doing
Your will
But my mind wants to do the will of this
world
To do things "the right way"*

Look at me,

Continually loosing my blessings
Doing things "The right way"
According to the world

Lord, I'm tired of loosing my blessing,
Staying stagnant unable to move
Because I'm out of your will.
I'm tired of this continuous struggle,
This seemingly permanent bondage
I've been living in.

Yes, Lord,
I know I haven't truly been living right

Not paying my tithes and offering,
humph, I'm so worried
About making sure everyone is this world
Is taken care of
I've forgotten to take care of
My first true love

I forgot to seek you first
I forgot or rather wished not to remember,
That it is because of Your blood
This captive has been set free.
I choose to overlook that blessing Your
kingdom
Actually blesses me and the many that will
come
After me.

I've chosen to forget that the love
You have for me Is everlasting.

*I've forgotten that my life is a
Gift that You've given to me*

*I've forgotten that your blood that was shed
healed
All my wounds, took away all my sins,*

And every one of my cares.

*I forgot without You
I can't move,
I stop breathing
My eyes cease to see
My ears no longer hear the sounds around
me.*

*Father, my heart is heavy, my mind is
crowded
My life has been turned upside down.*

*Lord, please help me!
Help me to be
That Woman of God,
You've shown me to be*

*Help me to be,
A testimony for
Those who struggle like me
Help me be a light,
that leads many souls to You.
Help me love like You love
Help me see as You see.*

Please decrease me so that You may increase.
Father, I know I've sinned and come
So short of your glory

But, Lord I ask You please
Help me to continue my story.
Let the legacy I leave have Your
Stamp of approval on it.
Let my children be set free from
Every curse that Satan has tried to create
with me and those he created before me.

Lord forgive me, I am a sinner and this my
prayer
Thank You for Your forgiveness, Your love
Your correction and Your compassion.
Thank You for listening to this sinner's
prayer.

Amen

Now Breathe!

A Change is a coming! Can you see it?
I can feel it deep down in my bones,
Straight to my spirit man!

Oh a Change is a Coming just you wait
and see!!!
Watch as the Change overtakes me!!